In the Footsteps of Explorers

Sir Walter Raleigh

Founding the Virginia Colony

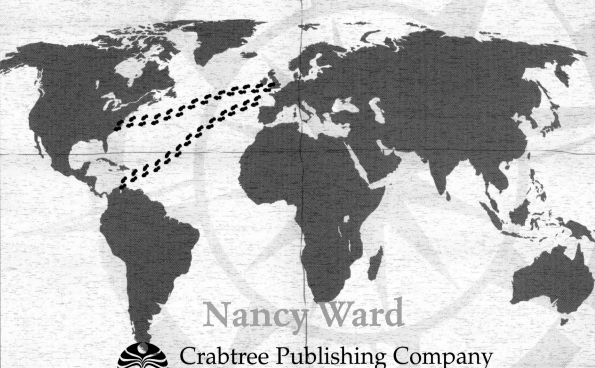

Nancy Ward

Crabtree Publishing Company

www.crabtreebooks.com

Crabtree Publishing Company
www.crabtreebooks.com

To my husband, Rob
- who believed in me even when I didn't believe in myself.

Coordinating editor: Ellen Rodger
Series editor: Carrie Gleason
Editors: Rachel Eagen, Adrianna Morganelli, L. Michelle Nielsen
Design and production coordinator: Rosie Gowsell
Cover design and production assistance: Samara Parent
Art direction: Rob MacGregor
Scanning technician: Arlene Arch-Wilson
Photo research: Allison Napier

Consultant: Stacy Hasselbacher, The Mariner's Museum, Newport News, Virginia

Photo Credits: Snark/Art Resource, NY pp. 12-13; Musee d'Archeologie et d'Histoire, Lausanne, Switzerland, Giraudo /Bridgeman Art Library: p. 10; Palace of Westminster, London, UK, /Bridgeman Art Library: p. 7; Private Collection, Archives Charmet/Bridgeman Art Library: p. 23; Private Collection,/Bridgeman Art Library: p. 5, pp. 8-9, p. 14, p. 30 (bottom right); Private Collection, The Stapleton Collection/Bridgeman Art Library: p. 30 (bottom left); Roy Miles Fine Paintings/Bridgeman Art Library: p. 26; Wallace Collection, London, UK,/Bridgeman Art Library: p. 30 (top); Raymond Gehman/Corbis: p. 11; Richard T. Nowitz/Corbis: p. 31; The Granger Collection: p. 15, pp. 20-21, p. 27;

The British Museum/Topham-HIP/The Image Works: p. 18; Mary Evans Picture Library/The Image Works: cover; North Wind Picture Archives: pp. 16-17, p. 19, p. 24, p. 25; pp. 28-29; Other images from stock photo cd

Illustrations: Lauren Fast: p. 6; Adrianna Morganelli: p. 4; David Wysotski: pp. 24-25

Cartography: Jim Chernishenko: title page, p. 22

Cover: One of the most popular stories about Sir Walter Raleigh was that he laid his cloak down for Queen Elizabeth to walk on so she would not muddy her shoes.

Title page: Sir Walter Raleigh sent an expedition to found an English colony in North America in 1584. He later went on voyages to South America in search of the legendary El Dorado.

Sidebar icon: A tobacco plant flower. Tobacco is a plant that is native to the New World. Raleigh's men found that the Native North Americans they met used tobacco in ceremonies. Raleigh is credited for making smoking popular in Elizabeth's court.

Crabtree Publishing Company
www.crabtreebooks.com   1-800-387-7650

Cataloging-in-Publication Data
Ward, Nancy, 1971-
Sir Walter Raleigh : founding the Virginia Colony / written by Nancy Ward.
    p. cm. -- (In the footsteps of explorers)
Includes bibliographical references and index.
ISBN-13: 978-0-7787-2424-7 (rlb)
ISBN-10: 0-7787-2424-7 (rlb)
ISBN-13: 978-0-7787-2460-5 (pbk)
ISBN-10: 0-7787-2460-3 (pbk)
1. Raleigh, Walter, Sir, 1552?-1618--Juvenile literature. 2. Great Britain--Court and courtiers--Biography--Juvenile literature. 3. America--Discovery and exploration--Juvenile literature. 4. Explorers--Great Britain--Biography--Juvenile literature. I. Title. II. Series.
DA86.22.R2W37 2006
942.05'5092--dc22

                                                    2005035752
                                                         LC

Published in the United States
PMB 16A
350 Fifth Ave.
Suite 3308
New York, NY
10118

Published in Canada
616 Welland Ave.
St. Catharines
Ontario, Canada
L2M 5V6

Published in the United Kingdom
White Cross Mills
High Town, Lancaster
LA1 4XS
United Kingdom

Published in Australia
386 Mt. Alexander Rd.
Ascot Vale (Melbourne)
VIC 3032

Contents

The Queen's Man

Sir Walter Raleigh was an English explorer, soldier, and poet. He is credited as the founder of the Virginia colony in North America. His attempts to establish a permanent settlement there failed, but paved the way for other English settlements.

Raleigh at Court

Raleigh lived during a period in history called the Renaissance, or "rebirth." During this time in Europe, art, theater, and poetry flourished. Raleigh was an extravagant man and his poetry and flattering ways impressed Queen Elizabeth I. A legendary story about Raleigh and the Queen tells that one day when Raleigh met the Queen out walking he threw his cloak over a puddle so that she could walk across without soiling her shoes. Raleigh served the Queen faithfully and she rewarded him with many positions of power and importance in her **court**.

(left) Sir Walter Raleigh was also an English privateer. This means that he was a pirate who was supported by the English crown. On Raleigh's expeditions, Spanish merchant ships were looted for their cargo, such as gold and spices.

Exploring North America

One of the privileges Raleigh received from the Queen was a **charter** to establish an English colony in North America. On the second expedition to Virginia in 1584, Raleigh's men landed on Roanoke Island, in present-day North Carolina. The expedition's captain, Arthur Barlowe, provided a report of what they found. In the report, Barlowe described the Native North Americans who greeted them.

"The rest of her women of the better sort had pendants of copper hanging in every ear, and some of the children of the king's brother and other noblemen have five or six in every ear. He himself had upon his head a broad plate of gold or copper, for, being unpolished, we knew not what metal it should be, neither would he by any means suffer us to take it off his head, but, feeling it, it would bow very easily. His apparel was as his wives', only the women wear their hair long on both sides and the men but on one. They are of color yellowish, and their hair black for the most part, and yet we saw children that had very fine auburn hair and chestnut color hair."

~ Captain Arthur Barlowe 1584

(left) John White was an artist who took part in Raleigh's expeditions to North America. His paintings show Native American dress, homes, and ceremonies.

- 1552 -
Raleigh is born in Hayes Barton, Devon, England.

- 1584 -
Raleigh sends his first expedition to Virginia.

- 1585 -
Second expedition to colonize Roanoke Island.

- 1587 -
Third attempt at colonization fails.

- 1618 -
Raleigh is executed.

- 1492 -
Christopher Columbus, (above) sailing for Spain, lands in the Caribbean.

- 1497 -
Explorer John Cabot explores the coast of Newfoundland for England.

- 1498 -
Portuguese explorer Vasco da Gama sails around the tip of Africa to India.

- 1576 -
English explorer Martin Frobisher searches for the Northwest Passage.

Europeans Set Sail

Since the late 1400s, European countries had been launching ships of discovery. Explorers, such as Christopher Columbus who sailed for Spain, had made important discoveries in the New World, or North, Central, and South America.

Carving up the Globe

In 1493, the Pope, or leader of the **Roman Catholic Church**, issued a **papal bull** that divided the world in half. Portugal was granted control of all new territories to the east of the line. This included the spice-rich islands of the present-day Moluccas, Africa, and India. All territories to the west of the line went to Spain. Spain's possessions included most of the newly discovered Americas, except for what is now Brazil, which went to Portugal. The Spanish and Portuguese were quick to establish colonies on their lands. From Spain's colonies in South America, Central America, and the **Caribbean**, gold and silver were added to the country's wealth.

Latecomers

France, England, and the Netherlands also wanted to gain wealth from trading in other parts of the world. Explorers from these countries believed that by sailing west across the Atlantic Ocean, they could reach the riches of China, India, and the Spice Islands and avoid Portuguese and Spanish territories. England was searching for a northern route to Asia called the Northwest Passage. Many explorers believed the Northwest Passage was a water route through North America that lead to the Pacific Ocean. Early explorers also reported unclaimed land in North America, and England and France were interested in claiming it.

(background) John Cabot was an Italian-born explorer. In 1496, England's King Henry VII granted Cabot and his sons support in exploring a northern trade route across the Atlantic. Cabot's voyages led England to claim what is now eastern Canada.

Elizabethan England

Sir Walter Raleigh lived during what is now called the Elizabethan Era. This was the period of time in England's history that Queen Elizabeth I was on the throne.

Religious Turmoil

Queen Elizabeth's father, King Henry VIII, established the Church of England, with himself as its leader. This broke England's ties with the Roman Catholic Church. The Church of England was a sect, or branch, of **Christianity** called **Protestantism**.

Many people changed their religion, or converted, from Catholic to Protestant. In 1553, Henry's Catholic daughter, Mary, became queen. During the reign of Mary, known as "Bloody Mary," 300 Protestants were tortured and burned at the stake. In 1558, Mary died and her half sister Elizabeth took the throne.

Reign of the Virgin Queen

Many people in England welcomed Elizabeth to the throne. During her reign, Elizabeth became a very popular queen. She ended the religious wars of Mary's time and **reinstated** Protestantism as the state religion. Her court was filled with loyal followers who flattered and admired her. Writers, musicians, and **scholars** were always in attendance at her court. Their artistic pursuits were encouraged and funded by the Queen. Elizabeth I was called the "virgin queen" because she never married. She provided her people with a stable **economy**, and the joys of artistic pleasures.

The Growing Empire

England had been weakened by Mary's reign and Elizabeth decided that by establishing ports and colonies in the New World, she could establish an **empire**. England entered into exploration as a way of challenging Spain for the wealth it gained from its New World colonies. The Spanish ran a profitable trade across the ocean. Some English sailors, called privateers, stole from Spanish ships and took the riches back to England. Wealth gained by the crown from pirating activities against the Spanish allowed England to fund more voyages and build colonies.

(background) Queen Elizabeth I had many suitors. Suitors were men who tried to win her hand in marriage.

Raleigh's Early Life

Walter Raleigh's father was a tenant farmer, which means he did not own his own land. Raleigh did not stand to inherit wealth from his family. Instead, he looked to his family's connections with important people in the court of Elizabeth to secure his future.

Soldier in France

In 1569, Raleigh volunteered to fight with the Huguenots in France. The Huguenots were French Protestants. In France, religious wars were raging between the Huguenots and Catholics. French Catholics feared that the Huguenots would take over the government. In 1572, thousands of Huguenots were killed in one day on the streets of Paris and throughout France. This became known as the St. Bartholomew's Day massacre. Raleigh narrowly escaped being killed in this event.

(below) Around 70,000 people were believed to have died in the St. Bartholomew's Day massacre in France.

Gilbert's Voyages

In 1578, Raleigh's half-brother, Humphrey Gilbert, received a charter from Queen Elizabeth I allowing him to set up English colonies in North America. Raleigh went with his brother on the journey and was captain of a ship named the *Falcon*. Three times the ships set out but storms forced them back to England. When they set out a fourth time, the *Falcon* sailed as far as the Cape Verde Islands, off the West Coast of Africa, before it was forced back. The Queen was not pleased with the expedition's failure. Gilbert and Raleigh were forbidden to sail again.

Fighting the Irish

Raleigh spent a short time in prison for his part in the failed expedition but was released in 1580. The Queen sent him to Ireland and gave him a post as **infantry captain**. England had established a colony in Ireland many years before and was trying to increase the English population there. The Irish **rebelled** against the English colonizers. The English squashed the rebellions, killing rebels in large numbers and burning their villages. Fighting against the rebels in Ireland provided a chance for Raleigh to prove himself and gain a personal introduction to the Queen.

(background) On July 30, 1583, Sir Humphrey Gilbert claimed what is now the Canadian province of Newfoundland for England.

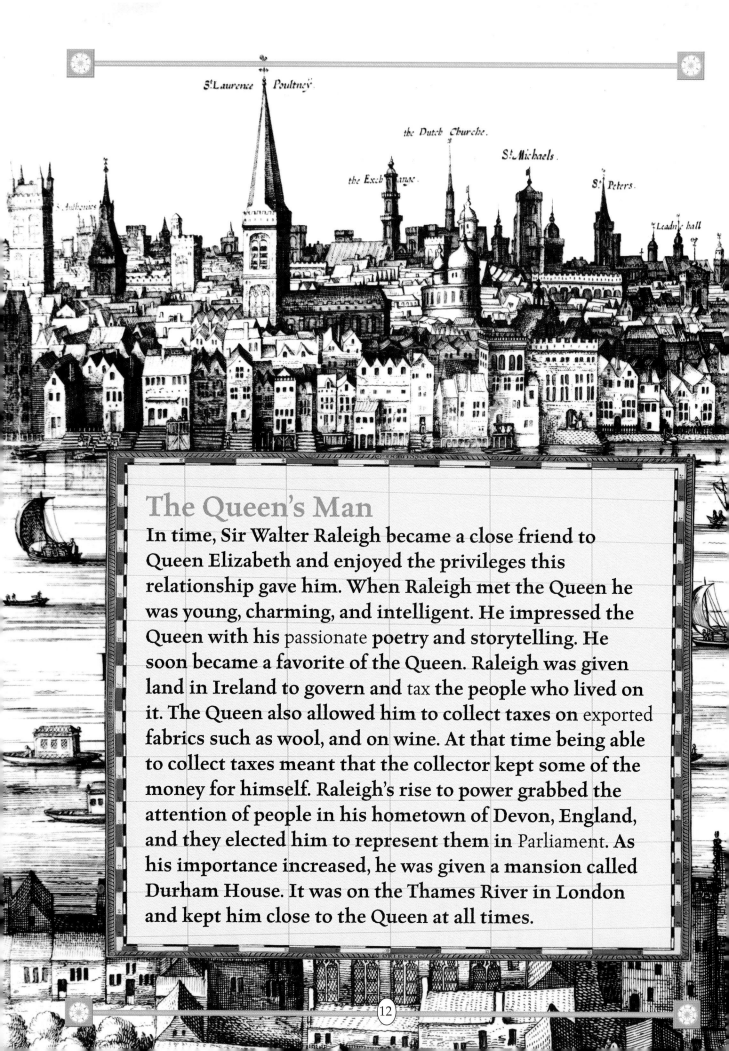

The Queen's Man

In time, Sir Walter Raleigh became a close friend to Queen Elizabeth and enjoyed the privileges this relationship gave him. When Raleigh met the Queen he was young, charming, and intelligent. He impressed the Queen with his passionate poetry and storytelling. He soon became a favorite of the Queen. Raleigh was given land in Ireland to govern and tax the people who lived on it. The Queen also allowed him to collect taxes on exported fabrics such as wool, and on wine. At that time being able to collect taxes meant that the collector kept some of the money for himself. Raleigh's rise to power grabbed the attention of people in his hometown of Devon, England, and they elected him to represent them in Parliament. As his importance increased, he was given a mansion called Durham House. It was on the Thames River in London and kept him close to the Queen at all times.

(background) An engraving from 1616 shows what London looked like at around Raleigh's time. The Thames River runs through the center of the picture.

St. Dunston in the east

Billing Gate

Bride Gate

The Virginia Colony

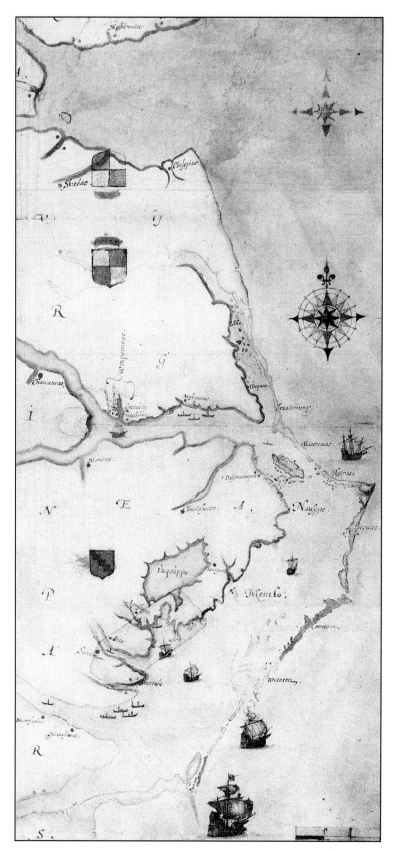

In 1583, Sir Humphrey Gilbert disappeared at sea on the return voyage from Newfoundland. Raleigh was granted his brother's charter to establish a colony in North America. To Raleigh's frustration, Queen Elizabeth did not allow him to leave to build the English colony. Instead, Raleigh was to organize the trip from England.

First Voyage of 1584

Raleigh's job was to organize the expedition and gather funding and supplies. Raleigh sent two ships to sail for the New World. Philip Amadas and Arthur Barlowe were chosen as captains. They sailed from Plymouth, England, to the Caribbean where they followed the coastline of Florida and eventually landed just north of Roanoke Island off the coast of North Carolina. Barlowe recorded the many discoveries they made, including an abundance of grapes, melons, fish, deer, hare, and fowl.

(left) John White was an artist on the second voyage to Roanoke Island. He made this map of the coastline of present-day North Carolina.

Contact With Native Americans

The Native Americans who greeted the English explorers were friendly, and provided feasts to welcome them. When the explorers returned to England, they brought two Native American men with them. One was Manteo, from the Native American Croatoan people. The other was Wanchese, of the Roanoke. These men were displayed in England in an attempt to raise funds for a colony. Raleigh and the Queen were pleased with the report of this land and it was named Virginia in honor of the virgin queen.

Second Voyage of 1585

A second expedition was planned to colonize the site at Roanoke Island. Raleigh's cousin, Richard Grenville, was chosen as the leader of about 600 sailors, soldiers, and settlers. Grenville's task was to take the settlers to Virginia and then return to England. Ralph Lane was chosen to lead the settlers after Grenville returned to England. During this expedition Wanchese and Manteo, the two Native American men who were brought to England, were returned to their homes.

(below) During Raleigh's time, Virginia covered almost the entire eastern coast of North America. Today, Virginia is a U.S. state. The Roanoke colonists landed in what is now North Carolina.

Establishing the Colony

As the second expedition approached the North Carolina coast, one of the ships, the *Tiger*, ran **aground** and lost all the **provisions**. The colonists needed the provisions to survive the winter. Once the expedition reached Roanoke Island, Ralph Lane, the colony's leader, started to build a fort. The fort was called "The New Fort of Virginia" and was located near the shore. Soon after, Grenville set sail for England on the newly repaired *Tiger* to get more supplies for the settlers.

Return to England

Many of the settlers at the Roanoke colony were soldiers. The soldiers provided the military power to defend against Spanish ships in the waters surrounding Roanoke. On Grenville's return journey to England, he looted a Spanish ship heavy with gold, silver, pearls, ivory, and sugar. The Queen and Raleigh met Grenville in England and were pleased with his loot. The Queen took a large portion of the stolen pearls for herself and Grenville split the ivory between Raleigh and himself.

Rescuing the Settlers

In North America, relations between the colonists and the Native Americans who lived near the colony deteriorated. Food and other supplies became scarce. The Native Americans had no more food to give the starving colonists and fighting broke out. One day, news arrived from lookouts along the coast that ships belonging to English privateer Sir Francis Drake were approaching Roanoke. Colonist leader Ralph Lane boarded Drake's ship and was offered supplies to last a month, or an immediate return journey to England. Lane did not want to give up on the colony, but realized the colonists might not survive if fresh supplies from England did not arrive soon. Two weeks after Lane and the colonists left Roanoke, Grenville finally returned. He found the colony empty. Grenville decided to leave 15 men to maintain the colony and supplies to last them two years.

(background) *Francis Drake was an English privateer who attacked Spanish ships. After defeating the Spanish sailors, he stole from them.*

- April 27, 1584 -
The first expedition departs from Plymouth, England for North America.

-September 1584-
Members of the first expedition return to England.

- June 27, 1585 -
Second voyage to colonize Roanoke Island departs.

- June 18, 1586 -
Sir Francis Drake returns Roanoke colonists to England.

Native Americans

Long before Raleigh's men arrived to colonize Virginia, Native Americans had been living on the land. The Native Americans that the colonists encountered belonged to the Algonquian language group. The tribes, or groups, included the Hatteras, the Roanoke, and the Chowanoc.

Meeting the Roanoke

On the first expedition to Virginia, the English met the Roanoke, who lived on Roanoke Island. Many different Native groups also lived in the area. Each group had a leader, called a werowance, or chief, and a territory where they hunted and lived. Differences between groups were worked out through ceremonies or battles. Some groups united to form larger groups for protection against an enemy.

(below) A painting by artist John White shows neighboring Native groups dancing at a meeting.

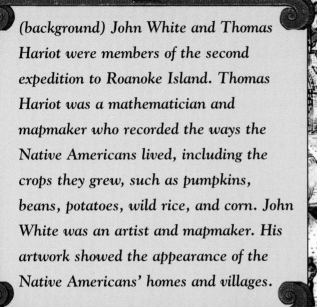

(background) John White and Thomas Hariot were members of the second expedition to Roanoke Island. Thomas Hariot was a mathematician and mapmaker who recorded the ways the Native Americans lived, including the crops they grew, such as pumpkins, beans, potatoes, wild rice, and corn. John White was an artist and mapmaker. His artwork showed the appearance of the Native Americans' homes and villages.

Corn Patties

Corn was one of the crops that Hariot recorded the Native Americans growing. Ask an adult to help you with this recipe for corn patties.

Ingredients:

1 cup (250 ml) yellow cornmeal

1 cup (250 ml) milk

1/2 teaspoon (2.5 ml) salt

1 tablespoon (15 ml) shortening

Directions:

Combine cornmeal and milk. Mix well. Add salt and shortening. Mix again. Drop batter by spoonfuls onto a lightly greased hot griddle. Turn when corners are brown and center is bubbly. Serve hot with butter.

The Lost Colony

In 1587, Raleigh organized another expedition to Virginia. This time the expedition included 150 men, women, and children. Some were planters and other skilled workers who would benefit a colony.

An Unfriendly Welcome

The colonists landed at Roanoke Island. When they arrived they found the fort burned. There was no sign of the 15 men Grenville had left behind. The colonists set to work to rebuild the fort under the direction of the **governor** of the colony, John White. The Native Americans that greeted them this time were less friendly than before. The Roanoke attacked soon after the English arrived.

War at Home

Near the end of summer, the colonists realized that they needed more supplies to last the winter. John White left Roanoke to sail home for provisions. While White was in England, Spain attacked England. A war broke out and White was forbidden to return to the colony. The colonists became less important at court than the war. White was finally able to return to the colony three years later.

The Disappearance

On landing, White found the settlement deserted and the houses destroyed. White found the letters CRO carved into one tree and on another tree CROATOAN. The overgrown grass told him the settlement had been abandoned for some time. No settlers were found, but the tree markings led White to believe that they had been taken by the Croatoans, a neighboring Native group. The fate of the colonists remains a mystery to this day.

(background) John White returned to the colony to find it deserted. White's young granddaughter, Virginia Dare, was the first English child born in North America. White did not know what happened to her.

- 1587 -
Third expedition to Virginia.

- August 18, 1587 -

Virginia Dare is born. She is the first English child born in North America.

- August 27, 1587 -

John White returns to England.

- 1590 -
John White returns to Virginia and finds the colony deserted.

The Fabled El Dorado

After the failed expeditions to Virginia, Raleigh turned his attention to other things. He secretly married and when Queen Elizabeth found out she flew into a rage and sentenced him to house arrest. Fallen from the Queen's favor, Raleigh's money and privileges started to run out.

A Legend From the Spanish

Raleigh remembered a story told to him by a Spanish explorer. The story was about El Dorado or "The Golden Man." According to legend, a king covered in gold ruled a very wealthy kingdom in South America. Raleigh wanted to find the kingdom so he could become rich and build an English base in Spanish-controlled Central and South America. He hoped accomplishing these feats would help him regain favor with the Queen.

Setting Sail for the Orinoco

Raleigh felt that the Orinoco was the best route to El Dorado. The Orinoco is one of the largest rivers in South America. It starts in Brazil and flows through Venezuela, where hundreds of rivers and waterways branch off into swampy land. In 1595, Raleigh left England and sailed for the Caribbean island of Trinidad. There, Raleigh burned down the Spanish town of San Joseph and captured its governor.

Trinidad

Venezuela

Guiana Highlands

ATLANTIC OCEAN

Voyage to South America

SOUTH AMERICA

Finding the City of Gold

Raleigh met the Warao people who lived on the Orinoco and realized he needed their help to succeed. He warned his men not to steal from or harm them. When the Warao chief killed one of his men, Raleigh responded by capturing one of the Warao to serve as a guide. The trip up the Orinoco River was made in extreme heat and humidity and Raleigh and his men suffered in the unfamiliar conditions. They discovered a country filled with colorful birds, brilliant flowers, and strange animals. When they found tools used to mine gold, they thought they were close to discovering El Dorado.

They traveled on to the Caroni River which led them into the present-day Guiana region of Venezuela. Smaller bands of men were sent out to explore. Battered by severe rainstorms, Raleigh and his crew eventually left for England empty handed. They did not find the city of gold.

(above) Raleigh wrote a book called **The Discovery of the Large, Rich and Beautiful Empire of Guyana.** *This illustration from Raleigh's book shows the legend he told of people who have no heads.*

Life of a Privateer

During Queen Elizabeth I's reign, England and Spain were enemies. The Queen gave licenses, called letters of marque, to English sailing ships. These licenses gave the crews permission to attack Spanish ships and ports as privateers and take bounty such as gold and trade goods. Both Raleigh and the Queen profited from privateering.

Types of Ships

Galleons were the most popular ships used by privateers. Galleons were large, heavy ships with three masts and three or four decks. Smaller galleons were built to be easy to maneuver in an attack. These ships were used in battles and for long voyages because they were durable, strong, and could carry many crew members. Large ships had **carriage guns** that protruded out the side of the ship. These fired metal or stone cannonballs. Smaller guns above deck could swivel to shoot at the enemy.

(below) John Hawkins was an English slave trader. In 1562, he captured a Portuguese slave ship and sold the African slaves in the Caribbean colonies. In 1569, John Hawkins became a privateer for Queen Elizabeth.

Sailor's Life

Life was hard for sailors. Their clothing usually consisted of a light wool or linen shirt or tunic and short pants that were worn day and night, every day. Sailors rarely wore shoes, and lice and fleas were common problems. Each day, sailors were given a small amount of ship's biscuit, salted meat or fish, and sometimes boiled peas or beans. Meals were cooked in the galley, or ship's kitchen, but when the sea was too rough it was impossible to cook for fear of setting the ship on fire. Ship's biscuit was a hard, dry, flat bread that stored well. By the end of a journey, most of the food had spoiled and sailors ate items such as maggot-infested cheese.

(left) The Bark Raleigh was built by Sir Walter Raleigh and had a sleeker design than the English ships before it. The ship had four masts and 50 guns. The Queen later bought the ship and renamed it the Ark Royal.

The Tide Turns

English privateers helped weaken Spain's naval power. After famous English privateers John Hawkins and Francis Drake died, England decided that the best way to check Spain's power was to attack Spain directly. Raleigh was one of the men chosen to lead an attack on the Spanish city of Cadiz.

Raleigh at War

(below) King James I tried to end England's long feud with Spain.

Five thousand English sailors, 65,000 soldiers, and three leaders defeated the Spanish galleons at Cadiz. Raleigh was injured when a cannonball hit the deck of his ship. His calf was reduced to shreds when he limped into Queen Elizabeth's presence and was reinstated by her.

The Queen's Death

Queen Elizabeth died in 1603. James I took the throne and took away all the important positions that the Queen had given Raleigh. Rumors circulated that Raleigh was involved in a plot against the King. Plotting to overthrow the King was a very serious crime called treason and was punishable by death. Raleigh was declared guilty and sentenced to death. At the last moment, the King pardoned, or forgave, Raleigh of this crime and locked him in the **Tower of London**.

The Prisoner

In prison, Raleigh wrote many poems and a book called *The Historie of the World*. He was also given a small room to conduct chemical and medical experiments. After 13 years, Raleigh was released by the King to lead one more expedition to find El Dorado.

Raleigh's Death

Raleigh was under strict orders not to attack Spanish ships or towns on the journey to El Dorado. When Raleigh became ill, his men defied his orders and burned the Spanish town of San Thome, which was located near the mouth of the Orinoco River. On his return to England Raleigh was arrested for disobeying the King's orders and sentenced to be executed for treason.

(below) On October 29, 1618, Sir Walter Raleigh was executed by beheading.

- June 11, 1596 -
Raleigh is involved in the attack on Cadiz, Spain.

- March 24, 1603 -
Queen Elizabeth I dies.

- 1603 -
Raleigh is imprisoned by James I.

- June 12, 1617 -
Raleigh leads another voyage to El Dorado.

- June 21, 1618 -
Raleigh returns to England and is arrested.

After Raleigh

Sir Walter Raleigh failed to establish a permanent English settlement in North America. Having learned from his mistakes, the first permanent English settlement later succeeded at Jamestown, Virginia. Raleigh also failed to find El Dorado, but he did prove to others that the kingdom of gold did not exist.

The Jamestown Colony

In 1607, while Raleigh was imprisoned in the Tower of London, Captain Christopher Newport led a colonizing expedition that settled at Jamestown, which was farther north along the Virginia coast than Roanoke Island. The land was swampy but suitable for settlement. The colonists traded with the Powhatan peoples who lived there, and tried to establish an alliance with them against their enemies. Farming was helpful to the colony's survival. By 1614, the colonists were growing tobacco and selling it to England. This gave the colony the staple crop it needed and more English colonists arrived and built settlements along the East Coast of North America.

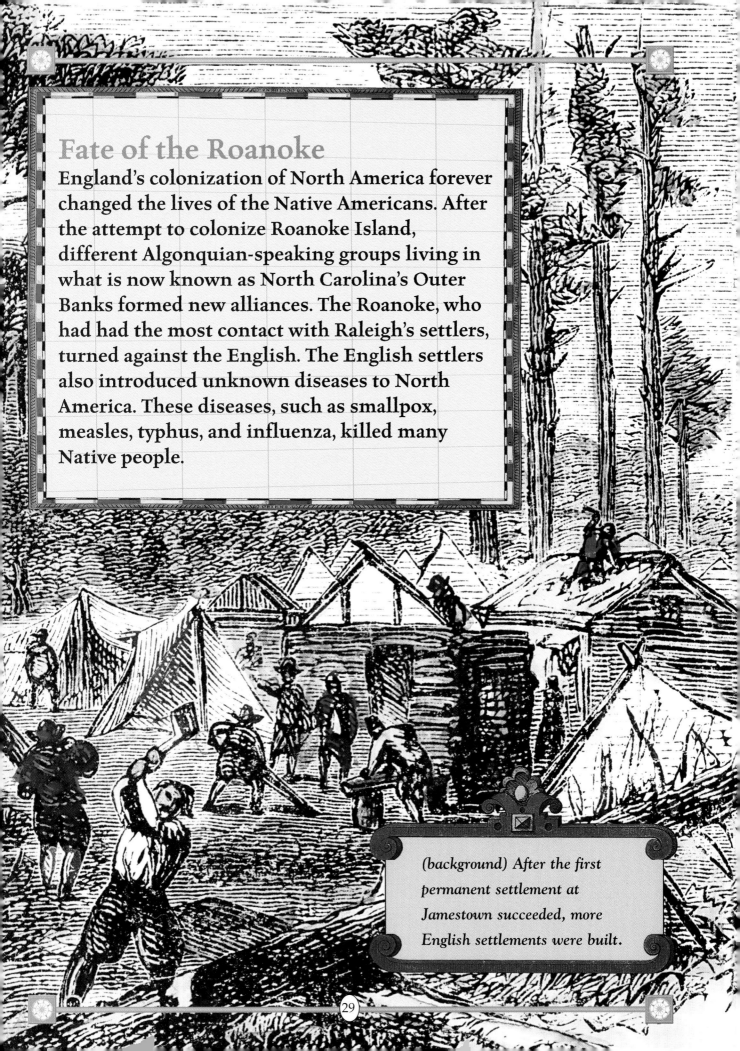

Fate of the Roanoke

England's colonization of North America forever changed the lives of the Native Americans. After the attempt to colonize Roanoke Island, different Algonquian-speaking groups living in what is now known as North Carolina's Outer Banks formed new alliances. The Roanoke, who had had the most contact with Raleigh's settlers, turned against the English. The English settlers also introduced unknown diseases to North America. These diseases, such as smallpox, measles, typhus, and influenza, killed many Native people.

(background) After the first permanent settlement at Jamestown succeeded, more English settlements were built.

Raleigh's Legacy

Many legends surround the life of Sir Walter Raleigh. Raleigh was a close follower of Queen Elizabeth I, but was disliked by many people during his time. Today, he is remembered for his writings, his attempt to colonize Virginia, and his voyages to South America.

Raleigh Myths and Realities

Raleigh is believed to have introduced potatoes and tobacco to England. Both of these crops came from the New World and were unknown to Europeans before their explorations in North, Central, and South America. Raleigh's writings tell what Elizabethan times and early colonization in South America were like. Raleigh's expeditions to North America allowed artist John White to paint some of the earliest images by a European of how Native Americans lived at the time. Today, North Carolina's capital city, Raleigh, is named after the Elizabethan explorer.

(above) A smoking kit believed to have belonged to Sir Walter Raleigh. Raleigh is credited for making tobacco popular at the English court.

(left) A page from Raleigh's The Historie of the World, *written while he was imprisoned in the Tower of London.*

(right) This painting by artist John White shows an Algonquian charnel house, or place where human remains are kept.

(background) The Roanoke lived in homes that were similar to the Powhatan yehakins in this Jamestown reenactment.

Glossary

aground To scrape along a reef, shore, or bottom of a river

Caribbean The islands between southeast North America and northern South America that separate the Caribbean Sea from the Atlantic Ocean. This area is also known as the West Indies

carriage guns Cannon mounted on heavy wooden frames that could be moved around a ship

charter A legal document that gives permission to rule over a land or service

Christianity A religion based on the teachings of Jesus Christ, whom Christians believe is the son of God

colony Land ruled by a distant country

court A king and queen and all those around them, including family, friends, servants, advisors, and officials

economy The money, goods, and services of a country

empire A number of territories or governments controlled by one country

export To sell to another country

governor The person appointed to rule over a territory or colony

house arrest Kept under guard and ordered not to leave the house

infantry captain The leader of a band of foot soldiers

inherit To receive money, property, or titles after a person's death

papal bull A charter or proclamation issued by the Pope, or leader of the Roman Catholic Church, to all of Christiandom

Parliament England's legislature, or law-making body of government

passionate Full of strong emotion

planters Owners or managers of large farms called plantations

Protestantism A branch of Christianity that broke off from the Roman Catholic Church starting in the 1500s

provisions Supplies, such as food and water

rebel The act of rising up against a ruler

reinstate To bring back to one's previous rank

Roman Catholic Church A branch of Christianity that focuses on traditional religious beliefs, practices, and rituals

scholars Well educated people

tax A government charge that must be paid

Tower of London A building complex in London, England that is officially a palace and fortress of the English king or queen. During Raleigh's time, it was also used as a prison

Index

1 2 3 4 5 6 7 8 9 0 Printed in the U.S.A. 5 4 3 2 1 0 9 8 7 6